Ai.
8.95

WITHDRAWI

LEARNING RESOURCES CENTER
SANTA FE COMMUNITY COLLEGE

EXPERIMENTAL LOVE POETRY

CHERYL CLARKE

Firebrand
Books
Ithaca, New York

WITHDRAWN

LEARNING RESOURCES CENTER
SANTA FE COMMUNITY COLLEGE

Other books by the author
  Humid Pitch
  Living As A Lesbian
  Narratives: Poems In The Tradition Of Black Women

Dedicated to the memories of my sweet nephew,
Najeeb W. Harb (1974–1989), and Black lesbians
Pat Parker (1944–1989), Mabel Hampton (1902–1989), and
Audre Lorde (1934–1992).

Earlier versions of some of this material have appeared in the follow-
ing books and periodicals: *Conditions, Feminist Studies, Hellas, The
Portable Lower East Side, Serious Pleasure* (Cleis Press), and the St.
Mark's Poetry Project journal.

Copyright © 1993 by Cheryl Clarke
All rights reserved.

This book may not be reproduced in whole or in part, except in the
case of reviews, without permission from Firebrand Books, 141 The
Commons, Ithaca, New York 14850.

Book and cover design by Betsy Bayley
Typesetting by Bets Ltd.

Printed in the United States on acid-free paper by McNaughton & Gunn

Library of Congress Cataloging-in-Publication Data

Clarke, Cheryl, 1947–
    Experimental love : poetry / by Cheryl Clarke.
      p.   cm.
    ISBN 1–56341–036–2 (hard : alk. paper). — ISBN 1–56341–035–4
(pbk. : alk. paper)
    1. Lesbians—United States—Poetry.   2. Afro-American lesbians-
-Poetry.   3. Afro-American women—Poetry.   I. Title.
PS3553.L314E96   1993
811'.54—dc20

                                      93–32509
                                         CIP

Contents

A Great Angel

Oh soul, a great angel moves deep as th'Atlantic
gorged with tongues.

Today she let me see two hundred shades of green.

A great angel, oh my soul.
Oh my moon and coal black sea.

Space
Invocation

I must get to those spaces:
black space of throathole
brown space of asshole
red space of cunthole
sex space of no turning back

Stomach
take me to them
and lead me in a good song

Living as a Lesbian Underground, ii

A faggot historian friend—once noted
now hunted—smuggled me the latest
in dyke fiction from Fiji.
I had to eat the manuscript
before I could finish it.

I was on my way underground when
uniformed children blondish forcing
my door nearly seized my journal.
I bribed them with adult books.
In a park a mustachioed gent in
trench coat no hat balding flashing
chased me for it.
(He recognized me from a photo in some old
literary review. It was a stunning photo.)
I outran him
and he yelled at me shaking his fists:

> "Hey, *poeta,* hope you have a good memory.
> Memory is your only redemption."

Hell I'm lucky.
I could be hiding some place
where I'm kidnapped
tortured on metal tables
fingers broken.
As it is my reveries have been confiscated
but my obsessions do me just as well.
Harder to manage and sexier.

An off-the-shelf mercenary counsels me:

> "Detention is like solitude, and
> don't poets need that? They'll let you
> have a western classic or two,
> a Norton anthology."

"Hell, what about a Portuguese-English dictionary?"

I ask as he pulls a leisure suit over his bush fatigues.

Around the time little Stevie Wonder's songs
were banned in the bantustans, a harried editor looked
up at me from my grazed manuscript,
shaking his head, said:

"Maybe in thirty years we can anthologize
an excerpt."

(Hell, I mimeographed the thing myself and gave it out in the
quarantine we used to call Park Slope.)

But hell I still don't know what it's like
to be blocked by bayonets and frisked for
The Color Purple or be forced to dance
around a bonfire while my favorite passage
from Pushkin burns before my eyes.

A whore who'd been detained and raped every day
for a month escaped to the red hills where
she encountered me and showed me a word
from a book
not my own:

"This word can get you violated,"

she said.

I'd never written the word.
But it was a good word.
It called me.
I had to write it or it would write me.
The pages of my journal were all written up
with words censored years before
they stopped selling blank paper,
pens, pencils, diskettes
(a few defectors had monitors).
I sneaked back into an old safe house
raided during the bombing of Tripoli.
I loosened a brick and pulled out
a suppressed manuscript
a tasty little piece
of interracial erotica
I'd written in the early days
of the emergency.
I wrote the word over and over
large and small on the back of every sheet
in cursive and in roman, in bold and fine.

I wrote it with my left hand
as well as my right.
I recited it every time I wrote it.
Played with my sex
as I wrote it
over and over.
And said it as I came
over and over

"Hey, *poeta,* memory is your only redemption."

Morgan Harris

The poetry poured out of her
when she cross-dressed,
she said.
(The poetry fairly poured out of her
anyway.)
She studied space;
learned to be spare and unsparing,
deftly metered,
slant,
subtle caesuras,
historical, hysterical.

She knows really how small everything is
and uses form to cut it further down.
Contexts never overwhelm her.
Humility is her way. And cigarettes.
Wine. Pleasures with women.
A rondeau and a sestina thrown in,
she penned a superb sonnet sequence
to just these subjects in her fifth book.
Morgan knows how small everything is.
Some greater depth.

To her, poetry is the smallest thing,
her greater depth.
Since before she wore glasses,
a frail funny-looking girl listening to the sound
of Joe Bataan
and dominoes,
imagining she could count the pips.

Prose Poems

i. This
This felt strong against me all day waiting for you and it. Days of ambivalence. Hours of eating. But today strong against, inside. This exquisite representation, its talents wasted on those who can't stay hard and can't take it off. This.

ii. Commerce
Act as if I fit in. It's best for protection. In this silly costume giving these people what they toss their coins for. I call for a *regular*, a *mayo on*, a *medium*. Nod through this stupid hat. Instinct and memory instead of conversation. The only words I know are essential. I am fluent in the language of their commerce. I know its value to its smallest part.

Stumbling on to the next commodity, they think I make a mistake or cheat.

iii. The No. 1 at 79th and Broadway
Going below. Looking up for a final glimpse of the Empire sky. But my bag, heavy, heavy with shoes. I carry the weight wearily. It forces my head down to see a strandy wad of wavy hair sticking to the step, its white roots and fading dye job.

iv. Hurricane Season
A woman lies on her back in the station restroom. Her hands at her sides. Her overcoat is new but her feet are grimy. She once had a beautiful mouth. I step over her.

When I come out of the stall men are kneeling around her trying for a pulse.

"I thought she was sleeping," I say to them.

"She's pretty dead," one of them pronounces as he strokes her brown cheek with a latex glove.

v. They Left
The two of them left. Almost overnight. Not two days' warning.

They'd raised many boys. Homeless, loveless, manless boys. Friends and uncles to many boys. Grieved the deaths of many nephews. Comforted a hundred sisters.

They left the city. Too little money. And angry children in gold jewelry. Too many woman-hating arsonists. Too much falling from great heights. Or money lenders? The law? The virus?

Over much quiet protest and loud speculation, they left.

vi. Turnstile
She is buggy, an old coffee cup asking for quarters at the turnstile.
She seems to be a boy. I know she, being both grown and female,
is pretending. I go along with her. She sometimes drools. I throw
her a quarter just to get her out of my sight some evenings. She takes
me every time.

vii. Testimony
The good wife who will die quietly. Mysterious, sexy, charming, obe-
dient. Then the needle. Ecstasy of fantasy. Anything for a fix. Even
the veins in my neck. Selling myself. Jail. Positive and six months
to live. Runaway.

The good wife who wanted to experience feelings. In the street, my
daughter crying over me. My 14K Miraculous Medal for the pipe.
And reckless fucking. Dangerous blood and cum.

viii. Bruce

He'd left D.C. sixty-three years before. A Renaissance man living out the memories in Hoboken. He'd stopped dyeing his hair. He was a frayed mulatto, dentures clacking as he chewed his Sunday eggs Benedict, yolk pooling at the corners of his mouth. (I wanted to give him my handkerchief.) Uneven traces of rouge on sunken cheeks. Bruce.

He removed the celery stalk from his vibrant Bloody Mary and sucked its flowery tops. His descriptions of *the* life were vivid. He'd been decidedly blasé. And was still so, except was now decidedly déclassé. Destitute. Still he gestured extravagantly and held his wrist like so. A shaman too. He'd known all the closets on Sugar Hill, and who was in them. Bruce.

ix. Dodge Ball

Gay. Black. Walking the streets like he got a right. And it's dark. And three teenage boys, black too, come up behind him. Play him like dodge ball. Put a snub-nosed piece to his head and he's back in Viet Nam. In a chorus, they tell him: "Roulette." They stop him in a chorus, too, on the count of three. Grab him again, play with him some more, and toss him down. They lope off without even a curse.

x. Peace, Queen

"Do you have vanilla incense?" I ask the black man stooping near the folding table on which lay a score of small cylindrical bottles, stacks of pastel literature, and brown bundles of stick incense.

Gleeful, he tells me, "Ask that beautiful brother over there, queen." I laugh and think of the golden days of Black Consciousness. Oh, sleepless nights of theory-talking. Months of discovering old truths. African cloths. The intensity of Lumumba. Trotsky eyeglasses. Kinky, curly, nappy, wild hair. Fanon. Fucking. Marijuana.

"Vanilla incense?"

"No sister," says the child whose black eyebrows meet in an arch. He seems almost fifteen.

"Are you Black?" I ask.

"Yes. And my father is from Damascus," he says patiently.

You will die soon, I think. "Do you have musk?"

He shakes his head yes and counts out the sticks studiously. Against my protest, he pours an oil into a tiny elliptical bottle, his fingertips and nails stained with his faithful commodities. He hands me the bottle.

"Give this balm to my mother," he says.

His black eyes hold mine, anguish firing.

"Peace, queen," says the stooping black man, who sees my ghosts.

xi. The C-Train Uptown

It's Sunday. The car's empty but for that bulldagger at one end and that wasted bum at the other. I'm feeling fine and this toothpick is tasting good, makes me smack my lips, sucking out what's left of breakfast. Good idea not to wear my jockeys. Oh, Lordy, nice. We're stuck between stations. Yeah! Loose this drawstring. My hand, my blessed hand. Yeah, this toothpick is tasting good. Getting horizontal now. Umm-humm. Just for me. That bulldagger's checking me out and wishing. Musta heard me sucking this toothpick tasting good. Here she comes looking lost. And me almost vertical. Shit.

"Yeah. This is the last stop, the end of the line! Lordy! This toothpick is tasting good!"

Saxen and Wilfreda

In a city of palm trees and highways
they appeared from the air.
The arid plains and the relentless concretes
had been fruitful for them.
Scholarships. Attention. Smiles from white folk
who said they had talent. They did have talent.
They were born with it.
One raised by aunts and first cousins,
the other by a brain surgeon and a school teacher.
They were good at everything.
And finer than fine.

In fact, the scholarships, attention, and smiles from
various and sundry white folk had brought them both to the
city of palm trees and highways,
predatory and longing for experience,
experimentation,
and good company.
Sick of being landlocked, they were.

"That's all there was on that concrete—
black and white. You were either black or white.
Nothing else," Saxen mused aloud.

"Least you had negro *and* white.
Wasn't nothing but white *or* nothing else
on that dry flatness," Wilfreda countered.

Drugs were plentiful then
and good.
You could trust a dealer to look out for you.
None of this copping on the street
or in doorways,
watching your back,
feeling for pockets.
Everybody was a farmer.
It was an easy time—
there was fraternity.
Men were still slime but easier to deal with.
Men truly made Saxen and Wilfreda appeciate women.
They could not wait to be in a double-deck Pinochle
game somewhere across the bay with some saucy sisters.
Away from the tutelage of certain fathers
they studied for form.

The white boys were gentler
but oblivious to stares in restaurants
while complaining bitterly of crumby seats.

"If those fools only knew.
I wish it stopped at not being able
to obtain the preferred seating," Wilfreda hissed.

The passing Saxen laughed under her hand
from the thrill of the waiter's confusion, and teased:

"If only you hadn't come,
my dark and comely,
we would've had our secret."

More and more they wanted to tell their own stories
in that misty land of cypress, redwood, and laughing seals,
running the streets nightly in search of jazz, poetry, and
tightening.

Once between men at the same time,
they noticed something about this
not-being-with-men that suited them both.
And they painted those spaces with broad brush strokes
of essential colors across the large canvases
that scholarship money bought.
Saxen would begin each day by writing a sonnet to herself.
Wilfreda sat in lotus.
Usually, one or the other would go to the room
of the other, bangles jangling,
scarves dropping,
barefoot,
clothes loose about the waist:

    "Got a story.
    Can you listen, now?"

The hum of the typewriter would stop abruptly
or the brush would drop to the floor
splattering points of scarlet acrylic.
The story would be received without censure.
By eleven they were ready to stroll through the city
to a hot tub.

The b-boys would return briefly
taking up space with their underwear.
The perpetually raised toilet seat.
The sonnets and lotuses disappeared with the mornings
lost in late-night seductions around horseshoe bars.
Wine-stained bedspreads.
Wax wrappers littering the floor.
Late mornings and unstretched canvases.
And lots of cold showers.

Mercedes, their dealer, advised:

> "Remember. This ain't the only vision, baby, ain't
> the only way to see that purple underside, that deep
> lore, taste the cloying juices."

Saxen and Wilfreda wanted that lore
and those cloying juices
bad enough to forego the b-boys.
(Once in a while, Saxen liked a little live dick.
Wilfreda happily satisfied herself with facsimiles.)

All the post-Bop music played relentlessly
through the terraces of their afternoons
to various altered states.

The infinite saxophone
signified them
in their solitudes.
Songs rose up
and lighted on the pages and poses of morning.
And the convergence was always inevitable
flowing toward the white water.

Ambiguity and talent are dangerous together.
Saxen and Wilfreda chose their archetypes,
the lure of their own subjectivities,
the open road, the stage,
the set, the back-up singers,
the crowd wanting truth
and them there telling
(their version of) it
to the movement of women
all night

till the final curtain call,
till those gamey leotards were peeled
off,
till the pills and all kinds of white and
brown powders, and sweet, sweet weed.

"Yes," quipped Wilfreda, in a near swoon,
"talent and skin color are stranger than
truth or fiction," as she sucked in the precious hash.

They were down for the convergences.

"Talent can go a long ways
with the right help.
Pops created modernism, didn't he?
Didn't Monk see beauty in fish scales," screamed the
dangerously thin Saxen, snorting whatever was passed to her.

Greta Garbo

Easter Sunday, April 15, 1990

I imagine you left Hollywood at thirty-six
because you had enough money to live as a lesbian
and didn't have to buy into heterosexuality
after Christina.

I imagine you overlooking the East River
or in Saks in fur coat
and sensible shoes asking,
"Please, do you have men's pajamas?"
A life of guarded anonymity, autonomy, alcoholism
all over Switzerland, the French Riviera,
and Italy wearing pants, flats, floppy hats,
dark glasses, and
toasting whiskey with an Alsace baroness
who liked it in the ass
yearly on the Rhine.

Cucumber

The texture of cucumber repulses my lover.
But last night we'd forgotten our toy.
I spied a deep-green firm cucumber
in our hostess' fruit dish.
I stole it to our room.
I made the room dark.
The drums outside became more than themselves
and syncopated.

I rubbed the perfect cuke with a ginger oil,
knelt near the bed
and lulled my eyes closed.

The toilet flushed.
Her steps.
The room filled with her sex
as she knelt upright before me
and faced me squarely,
hazel eyes searing the brown dark.

Anchoring myself against her with one hand
and with the other pulling aside the crotch
of her bathing suit.
And felt her there.
Bent and put my face there
to make certain of wetness.
She was surprised at first by
the coolness of the lube,
but I assured her she could take it.
Soon she had no question, even talked to it.

   "I finally learned a way to make you eat me,"
   I spoke back in a voice not my own.

Movement

i.
I was a brown ball of a chap
when a small light-skinned Negro working woman
refused to give up her seat to a white bus rider.
Three months after, my father took me to our new church.
Surveying from a distance, I said, "How pretty,"
to those pastel dots of white people.
My father said, "Hush, girl."
I'd been taught the *Baltimore Catechism*
by cinnamon-faced Oblates of St. Thomas the Moor.
This would be my first mission.

ii.
His first mission was Alabama.
The cotton bolls sway in the gentle dusk breeze.
Soft is the welcome darkening.
The evening star signals a tenuous freedom and workers
sing toward the Wednesday prayer meeting
eager for the spirits.
A woman with one breast and thick plaits is overcome
by the refrain, *Walk, children, don't you get weary.*

iii.
Walk, children, and don't get weary
before you get to Mississippi.
It was rough, Mississippi.
People got killed
and maimed regular.
We learned to drive fast at night.
One night not fast enough.
Three of us.
Driver didn't die though shot in the neck.
The two of us got him to a hospital
and sent a telegram to the President.

iv.
The President never understood the Civil War
that year I played alone at recess.
Boys on one side of the yard.
Girls on the other.
A nun at either end.
The boys' nun was five feet tall,
solid, and swarthy.
She spun like a top on her
thick black heels
when the boys tugged at her veil.
She was aloof from them though. And stern.
We surveilled one another the whole hour of
blue-grey play.

The girls' nun was giraffelike
and moved her brown lashes up and down
in blue-eyed laughter at
the girls gathering around her
for a touch, a word, a favor.
Her eyes sought mine every day
just above their heads of flowing hair
always just before the bell rang.

v.
Always just before the almsgiving
he was overcome by the burden of the love
people gave back to him.
He spoke from a familiar text that extraordinary night,
handkerchiefs signaling the anticipation,
the joy of victory.
Finally, he fell back from the pulpit
full with it
into the arms of his angel.

vi.
No guardian angel could protect
this light-skinned black boy
in our school that had the last name of Nixon.
His light-skinned black father, my dentist,
was voting for Nixon the first time
D.C. voted for a President.
The nuns pushed Democrats.
Kennedy called Coretta King
and every Negro in D.C. voted for him,
except Nixon's father.

vii.
Nixon's father was Edna Dockings' dentist, too. Edna Dockings was
our piano teacher. A birdish woman with bony, veiny, rubbery fingers
from years of abusive practice. Mrs. Dockings was full of uplift sto-
ries, a graduate of Oberlin, and a Yankee. While she drilled us in
her basement studio on Schirmer's Library, she read us her grand-
mother's letter from a great-aunt who drove off slave catchers regu-
larly with stones. She called all three of us "Baby Sister."

Mr. Dockings, "Daddy," practiced a monotonous cello from the third floor and smoked a dirty pipe. He called Mrs. Dockings, "Edgy." While my two sisters received their lessons in the basement, I was made to practice exercises on the faulty but sumptuous grand upstairs. Daddy would stop his practice, come down, and ask me to play Mozart.

viii.

Ask me to play Mozart and
imagine me being beaten in my face by a white man
until my eyes are lopsided
because I used a restroom
or sat at a counter
or drank from a water fountain.
Symbols are leaden.
Somewhere in Mississippi,
a black man is made to beat you until he tires.
A white man beats you some more.
You laying on your stomach,
trying to keep your dress down,
screaming.
The white man whispering close to your ear,
"Black bitch, big ass, you better shet up and be still."

ix.
I couldn't shut up and be still
whenever I was near Xavier,
my best friend.
I dreamed of sleeping with her before
the relentless pressure.
Her father, Pinky, let her drive his Dodge.
Xavier was a self-hating mulatto,
always trying to pass,
but her nose was too broad.
I loved her.
The memory shames me.

x.
That memory shames me, but then I remember
how my mother and her light-skinned lady friends loved
books and politics.
They read *Lady Chatterley's Lover,*
Tropic of Cancer,
Pinktoes,
Light in August,
Another Country.

The Negro in American Culture was the subject of a hot discussion
over a Pokeno game one Sunday.

xi. The Interview
"Even on Sunday slaves didn't deserve rest, sir.
Rather unworthy, slaves.
Not adequate.
No real powers of discernment.
No souls.

"A slave could be sick
her water breaking
feeble-minded
or six years old,
yet made to do unrelenting hard work
any time night or day,
sir."

"Though I was never treated cruelly,
I saw dastardly things done to others
for the slightest lack of measure.
A slave could be triced up to a tree and get
a hundred lashes and then be washed with brine;
or made to drink a strong medicine,
put in stocks, foul on himself, and be left
there for up to two days.
I saw a woman once. She cooked in the house.
Her mouth was locked with an iron muzzle."

xii.
The image of the iron muzzle stays with me. We should have stayed
in Manhattan. But we let the nuns persuade us to return to D.C. with
the rest of the class. It was a cold day and cops on horses were all
about as surges of people covered Fifth Avenue. Scorned by the
Movement, he walked at the head of the march. The sadness of the
bus ride back and the loss of freedom. Then: married and caught
in the quicksand; then out with barely the clothes on our backs. The
year of my divorce I slept with an ex-nun wearing men's underwear.

Summer of 1973

Right after I witnessed a phalanx of black lesbians
give a panel on gay liberation,
I fell in love with a spinsterish butch
of a black woman with a Scandinavian first name.
We chased each other every night
all over the West Village,
cruising every woman that walked or rode.
She knew the Upper West Side like the palms
of her talony hands.

We would sit in a subleased apartment
on Columbus Avenue playing double-deck Pinochle
with two other bulldaggers
for three days straight.

My whole summer was bulldaggers, spinsters,
generous femmes, dark butches, and loud-talking lesbians.

Committed Sex

Bump the Supreme Court and Edwin Meese
I'll read anything, do anything to be sexually aroused
I'll be a lesbian, queer, whore, a sleaze
and it won't be a peep show that I ain't caroused.

Steal a camcorder, make my own videos to be sexually aroused
to get my mind off star wars and other wars
and it won't be a massage parlor I ain't caroused
to dance with my own kind, to flash my ass to the stars

To get my mind off CIAs, contras, and other wars
in Beirut, Belfast, Sharpeville, Philly
to sleep with my own kind naked under the stars
to pose in a harness, to kiss her pussy

In Tegucigalpa, La Paz, Luanda, Miami
we gon bend down and tickle our asses
and straddle her face and lick her pussy
we'll fight like wolverines for our asses

We gon bend over stick our fingers in our asses
no closets, quarantines, kitchens, Calvin Kleins
we'll fight like guerillas for our asses
like a Viet Cong, a Sandinista, for all time

No camps, bantustans, monogamy, Calvin Kleins
like a rebel slave or rebel Comanche
like SWAPO, the PLO, the ANC for all time
we'll watch any scene, play any part we fancy

Like a wild maroon, like a two-faced mammy
down with Supreme Courts and Edwin Meeses
we'll fuck, suck any genital we fancy
we'll be lesbians, queers, whores, sleazes.

passing

i'll pass as a man today and take up public space with my urges in the casual way he does in three-piece suit and gucci pumps big pants and large sneakers tight jeans and steel-tipped boots read my newspapers spread-eagled across a whole row of seats make my briefcase-boombox-backpack into an ottoman on the seat across from me on the l.i.r.r.; and spread my legs from here to far rockaway on the mighty i.n.d.; and when i get sleepy or bored spreading the brim of my blue fedora on the bus to queens hunch down cross my fat feet into the aisle and lean forward with my arms folded into the great press of rush hour flesh, hawking, spitting, and pissing all the way.

All Souls' Day

And we are in a bad way, directions uncertain.
How would we see the souls?
Afraid of each other but wanting our deaths;
and war threatening in some far-off bedroom.

This catacomb is a carnival of survival marvels
and language and no unhampered passage.
Their costumes tattered
matted hair
funny shoes
dirty legs
masks of tabloids and brown paper bags.
We embrace them in our anger at each other.
They are sucked back into the tunnel.
Half-masked we skip out onto the street
laughing at our little triumph.
pretending we have no history
no sordidness
no deaths
and maiming
have never known the little girl
who got a block of wood
forced in her small mouth for crying.

Flowers of Puerto Rico

. . . Last night my table was adorned with roses,
although I did not get one cent for my lecture.
                                        Frances E.W. Harper (1878)

i. Cruz de Martha
What or who is Martha's cross?
Lazarus sealed in a tomb but not dead?
The daily sorrow of her sister Mary?
Jesus' heat and desperation to roll back the stone?
("Behold how he loved him," whispered the gossips.)
The putrid smell of a recent corpse?
Her own longing for the Body?

Indians, impressed by the miracle of Martha's longing, named the
yellow, red, and pink blossoms Cruz de Martha to mark their sur-
vival of the Resurrection.

ii. Reina de las Flores
Draping trees with purple,
you are the robe of Iphigenia,
whose father was signified to death
by that color for his murderous hubris,
Reina de las Flores.

The reckless Clytemnestra
drapes the purple robe over Agamemnon,
bloated from conquest.
How could she sleep with him
even out of duty
after such a treacherous sacrifice
to appease the absent winds of Aulis?
After her own pact with Eros?

She prayed for the return,
and cultivated the moment,
gave herself up to its final paradox.

    "She was my daughter. Her death was my death,"

said the queen as the knife drew closer.
Reina de las Flores,
the robe of Iphigenia,
the lies of mothers.

iii. Flamboyan
Bold flamboyan, flashing:
a spray of passion,
beads of blood from a crown of rosethorns,
or a rare refraction
of the sun?

Conceit

You refuse to visit me.
You are no proper neighbor.
The house is dark where you live.
Mornings and afternoons you seem to be
on other errands.
And I don't pursue you.
I let you remain
on the other side of the door.

On my side of the door
in my part of the house, I give in
to my drab fear
without even touching myself
a poor substitute anyway
for your hospitableness.
A dry death is poetry
without you.

A Child
I Saw Myself

A child I saw myself not brave but full of terrors
entering mountains where dried
or pulverized bones, grinding stones, rusted
chains encircled my frail fire.
A precious and dangerous literacy as a child I
saw myself excavating.

A child I saw myself seated and working.
My dreams became blessed with images of trees
and the stark sun of March.
I taught myself how to be alone.
And soon there were no dreams
only the soon-filled blank canvas
the plucked strings
and anxious, awkward composings.
I shaped myself then as I would be
as I am now
working with my fingers
this too-elusive urge,
its sometimes clayey texture.

Buttons

I wanted to unbutton every piece of your clothing
which was all buttons
from that silk shirt
down to the crotch of that gaberdine skirt.
My buttons too:
my jeans brass-button up,
my shirt has six shell buttons,
my camisole has three tiny ones.
This restaurant is in my way
when I want to be unbuttoned
and unbuttoning.
Can't you tell?
To do it now.
To reach across the bread.
To start unbuttoning.
My arms so long.
My fingers faster than the eye and omnidextrous.
Now, ain't that loving you?

interlude

late drinks
late talk
and a perfectly timed split
opening against
sheer blue-sheathed calf
denim desire
rough   tight
ass against crotch
seamhard.
oh, clothes and the clothes you cover
till skin
till hands vanilla as can be
motion toward all zippers
among the xerographic
and foolscap
untutored   groping light switch
and moving consensually
to undo frontal closures,
proud to be easy.

Bergamot

Come now, and let us reason together...
though your sins be as scarlet...

Isaiah 1:18

I saw a wild bergamot,
crimson on your forehead
the laden afternoon you came
from her going away party
two nights before.

An Epitaph

Of Mabel Hampton. Pride.
Heritage. Girlfriend. Butch.
At the top of her Bronx stairs
frying fish.

Riding the running board
of an antique Ford
on Pride Day.

Years of ancient Pride:
    Runaway.
    Hoofer.
    The lucky bus stop.
Perpetual shrine to forty years.

Of Mabel Hampton in audiences
peering through dark lenses.
Soulmate.
More peerless.

Rondeau

They are bodies left unburied.
Instead of roaming the underworld, they've tarried
to bring their nomadic anxiety
to my world with little propriety.
I'd rather them waylaid in Staten Island, unferried.

Sit next to this one here, pass her, there's that one there.
This one's pretty, that one tall.
Her there, she's fair.
Haunt my solitude, hurt my silence, make me crazy.
They are bodies.

I try to act modern, but still I'm worried.
We sleep together every night and still I'm worried
that she or she loves you more expertly sexually
than me obsessed by her or her like voices of insanity.
Provocative and sexy nonmonogamy in theory.
But they are bodies.

Make-up

i.
If I were to paint myself for you
I'd paint my skin like a Nubian.
I'd do it at dusk by a bright fire.
I'd squat like the Nubian
genitals revealed and flaccid.
First the henna.
Then the ochre.
Then the ash.
Your breathing would quicken.

ii.
I remember my mother painting herself mornings.
The exact applications of powder, rouge, mascara.
She had passions and mostly obsessions, my mother.
And peacock ink etchings staining her fingers, the
ledgers and looseleaf.
Evenings she spent before the canvas painting to mute
the sound of the day's cadenced relentless supervision.
Make-up was her art
like the Nubian.

iii.
We are all three naked:
the artist, you, me.
Let her tattoo the dream of a perfect design
the dream of sunrays.
Let her make it a perfect cicatrix.

I watch her with the needle.
You are brave as the ink takes hold,
as the blood comes to the surface.
The sun is belligerent.

Remember
the Voyage

for Noel DaCosta

Remember the voyage,
the leaving, the theft of mangoes.
The poorly tuned but graceful fiddle
haunting Harlem school days.
The small parlor.

Remember the breadfruit and ancient marketwomen
marking their places,
gapped-tooth women of the calabash,
whose hands were always busy
even after purple dusk cooled equatorial sun.
Remember mountains singing in the Caribbean,
and the blue twilight of Harlem melting into bawdy moon.
The blood.
Remember the Etruscan ruin
and fingers seasoning unplucked strings.
Remember the calabash.

Berdache

I have always had a place with my people.
A sacred tipi adorned with feathers and bones.
An ancient rite I practice in subway stations.
One hundred years have passed since my tipi was sealed.
I wear the clothes of my sex
except on certain christian holidays.
My rite is suppressed.
But I know how to do it.
And will.

A Poet's Death

A poet's death and sex thoughts rode me
through the flashing December hurricane.
My day was spent traveling in circles
to get somewhere aboveground.
I had a straight-ahead goal when I woke up.
The floods altered it quite a bit.
I didn't get there.
Only got as far as the corner.
The winds and no available cabs
made me turn back.
And I was unfulfilled in the afternoon that followed.

All day long your words fought against my forgetfulness.
They became beasts with sharp bites.
In the distance cars on the FDR were sucked into the East River.
Cum residues sucked me back into thoughts of you.
And you, floating somewhere over the Guinea Coast
or some other blood-anointed place.
And you stuck in Brooklyn,
trains out.

The trains were running by the time I needed to ride
them, and, oh, what a Dutchman's ride they were
with absolutely no service to Far Rockaway.
I did not have to get out of Brooklyn either
and patiently passed the crisis underground.
My addictions tickling me through several stations.
I tried to memorize a poem by Whitman to get my mind
off sugar.

Audre, my good neighbor,
I miss your elegy,
your so-long song.
Long rhythmic lines of striking metonyms.
A raging narrative to recall your hermetic lineation.
Raw and grand images breaking splendidly
and turning to new space.
Spare like headlines or epitaphs.
My loveliest, my darkest, my most voice.
I miss my voice, my tongue, my most voluptuous lips.

You are in a different weather zone.
The airports are closed here
and everybody who's got a home
has been advised to stay in it.
Unless, like me, there is contraband you really need.
Really needy me
and denying it all the way uptown.
Totally oblivious of the fact
that a thirty-eight-year-old woman
was killed in Jersey City
when struck by a gutter propelled by the winds.
You thought it might have been me.
It might've.

A poet's death and the smell of cunt
rode me like the angels of hell
on the underground
today
traveling in circles
looking for
vague space somewhere
just ahead or just behind.

Arroyo

All week long the Sandias watched me.
I couldn't shake their stares:
mist-covered morning stares,
red-and-gold evening stares,
hanging white cloud day stares.
I drove into them fiercely
to pierce their awesome body
to pick through my own bones.
They received me.
Like you in another range
further north
named for the blood of Jesus.
There was no blood but kinship between us.

I am not a mountain to stand for millennia
to stare at nakedness
and be naked too.
I was very north
and you asked me to go farther.
I prefer the arroyo,
to receive the floods
that sometimes drown,
to be taken south.

Dear One

Why take so long to ask for it?
Come on, girl, are you gonna go after it?
Two days.
I'm only here for four.
Must you be courted so?
Your lovely breasts want
to linger over me.
It's pouring out of you.
I called you weeks ahead
so you could free yourself up.

You bragged that you'd risk the taste
of a stranger's juices,
so committed to desire's destination,
your mouth, the flow of menses.
But you won't take the first step with me.
I have to undress you, undress myself,
pull down the bedclothes,
push you between them,
get on top of you,
stretch the latex, and
talk you through it.

I been traveling to you for four years
from a desperate place
of grimy concrete and oxidized bronze.
I'm tired of assumptions.
Can't you just enter, kneel,
and make me first?
That's why I picked you.

Dykes Are Hard

Dykes are hard
to date.
A dyke wants commitment,
romance without abatement,
and unrelenting virtue—
all before the first show of flesh.
While you, a dyke too (and also hard
to date),
may only want to fuck her,
tell her she's got a nice
back, touch her pussy, talk dirty,
she's got another whole agenda.

Dykes should break loose and put off
monogamy, pregnancy, permanency.
Pack your rubber, latex, and leather,
and go on the make.
I know we'll hook up somewhere.

Tortoise and Badger

I'll still follow, primordial
thing, out of the swamp to the vague median
and beyond. Your shell is hardly cordial
and my spiky fur has gone seedy

with the strain of another defenseless fight
with you, your sparse hairs under my claws.
Want to tickle the back of your chelonite
and squeeze your small snout in my paws.

Want to turn you over to your soft belly,
silly, hungry me. You don't have much meat.
Just layers of sad and pleading, scaly
skin. Finally, I'll kiss your dancing feet.

You can scuttle all you want down the trail.
I'll still scurry right behind and bite your tail.

Living as a Lesbian at Forty-Five

Oh, it's a frequent dream:

He (He?) comes home hot and
wanting too.
You're in your room and wanting too
but wanting to control and orchestrate
so you can get it without really
acknowledging it will have a past
this
one way or another
in concert or in solitude
late
your juices built up from the day
odors sanguine
in the mood to take yourself
you set your works and toys out
and him
even though he knows you're a lesbian
there are those times
he still loses his crotch
in the part of your ass through your dress.

And that's how it happens
and it doesn't happen just once
and you may have work like poetry
to do like now and it starts
making you
pay it
some attention
and you run
and get your accoutrements
in excessive solitude
and space ephemeral with wetness.

Future Orientation

I always start naked, supine or prone.
Desperate stumbling for passion makes me panic-
ky. I can do without perspiration.
No cold fish nor kinetic
mammal. I risk the heretic-
al stance of future orientation
without guilt, apology, or ingratiation.
I will not look foolish for sex.
I plan.

Najeeb

(1974–1989)

The last Sunday
I saw you,
you were so brilliant with light
I could not see your face.
You'd grown taller than me
and were clumsy in your new height
choosing to wear your denim jacket indoors.
Loving your new adolescence, excited by the prospect
of years of growth ahead:
Would you care for me in my old age?
Did I have a right to expect that,
being only an aunt?

Instead I should have held you until you broke away
and even as you broke away.
As it is I cannot remember if I
even touched you as you left
that last Sunday.
You were so brilliant with light
I could not see your face.

Choking

Last night
I saw how I would die
by choking.
I would be by myself
mesmerized by cable
in bed with a bad cold
smoking reefer
and cigarettes
and coughing
coughing
not able to get my breath
unable to scream for help
by myself
and I'd die like that
sort of frozen in the horror of it
my mouth and eyes open.

Sadness

I used only to feel a sadness after.
Now, you are so elusive the sadness shrouds
the foremoments.
Suddenly, I feel you, a bright and
tinseled sparkling inside me.
Your sharpness dims
and I'm clutching only that drab fear.

Prayer

Why can't I want you?
(Or is it you who don't want me?)
Are you gone again?
Or is it me gone?

No rush of feeling
in that formidable place of violet sentinels
when I open my eyes.

Two years ago
you gave me a sign
to pull back from pretenders.
I'm still pulling
and so are they.

But can we be friends?
Is there no rush of feeling
nor vague chance
we might meet each other again
in that formidable place?

Gabriel

for Noel DaCosta

Gabriel moves through this maze
of me, this diaspora of virtues,
a poetry unwritten crazi-
ly resonating around the pews.
The curlicues of old-time anthems
mock the master's heavy rule,
its precise tyranny, its cant hymns.

Voices lift and multiply, a glossalalia of cruel
histories without the drum. But hand claps
keep forbidden time for all time.

And my Gabriel sits on every lap,
and slants and breaks every rhyme.
And loudly vamps it.
And loudly vamps it.
Oh, Eshu.

Untitled

i.
How much I do want you
all the time   for my
self   never out of my
legs   nights pushing
between your thighs is
relentless, infinite waking,
primordial   nights without
you   dark is sorrowful   mornings
forgetful of dreams.

ii.
For me I want my body's
freedom to protect the narrowness
and breadth and danger of
my own bed.

On Your
Forty-First Birthday

for E.W.

We make our witness in the world, friend.
Tonight we sleep apart neither dreamless
nor passionless: fearful of what portend
our futures. War, sickness, madness seem less
contained, and encroach upon our beds
in our separate hungry cities with cups
of hope. We give loose change against the dread,
grim predictions of a woman who sups
a moldy crust of pizza, inhaling toxic fumes,
and blessing the bus with her stump of hand.
Every street is an unmarked grave, a tomb
for whales beached on Long Island Sound.

But you are forty-one today, dear friend.
And this poor sonnet sings to you through the sand.

Veronica Ashley Wood, My Niece

(b. December 10, 1990)

Welcome, Veronica Ashley Wood.
Vision of god.
Truth.
Your beautiful ten-day-old lips.
What dreams after pain of birth?
We watch you. Feed you.
Pass you among us.
Cry and laugh at your frailty
and the character of your hands.

Hanging Tough in the Persian Gulf

Pvt. Adrienne L. Mitchell, a twenty-three-year-old Black woman with a dream, paid a heavy debt for wanting a college degree. Pvt. Mitchell had a goal: a career in law enforcement. She signed up in the Army and deferred her duty until she finished her degree. The Gulf War cancelled that deferment, and Pvt. Mitchell found herself in a makeshift barracks in Dahran, Saudi Arabia, unprized and unknown.

What do mainframe imperialism and a degree in law enforcement have in common? The uniform? In a place nobody knows your name or only knows you as enemy, though history and dark skin make you kin? Pvt. Adrienne L. Mitchell, of Moreno Valley, California, didn't your father tell you he'd lend you the money as he cursed the ball-less wonders on the Hill?

But wasn't Dad a thirty-year veteran and never had a scratch? (And then there was Colin Powell.) That was good enough for you, Adrienne L. Mitchell. You didn't bank on a sho-nuff war, in a make-shift barracks, fodder for that Scud the Storm Troopers couldn't cancel. After all you were the daughter of a thirty-year veteran, just trying to pay for a college degree, how could this be?

Elegy

for Donald Woods
December 18, 1957–June 25, 1992

I loved your brown grace and mauve words
from the first night I heard you through
the mist in a Manhattan auditorium.
So like the young redwood, growth inevitable,
its passionate powers,
a poet whose comeliness
I will no longer be able to wrap my arms around.
I fall to pieces and still want your promise
and the sound of your slant voice.
I am not resigned.
You were too quiet.
You sang too low.
How prized if not known?
What would I have done had I known?

Heartache

Your breasts visited me in a reverie,
facelessly, two friends,
and sat with me till the dailiness imposed itself.

an old woman muses from her basement

there's absolutely no reason (in the world)
nor no need
to go outside again.

i've kinda hoped for this
leveling
to nobody and nothing.
it seems the only honesty possible
without heroes.
rather shabby.
tacky.

no reason (on earth) to go out
unless any of them that's left
outside
comes in here.
ain't likely.
but lord knows i got enough down here
to stock a hotel for a month.
but i'll miss the little runs
papa took me on in the sedandeville
to the safeway.

least i'm beginning to pick up static
on the tv

and papa just went the first thing.
i sewed his easy body in the sheet,
dragged it out to what was his garden.
i look out on him
the sheet more shrunken each day.

me—divorced, two children, the depression,
roosevelt's death.
the death of billie holiday.
no electricity to no electricity.
i always knew it was all a bum steer.

down here
and old bicycles squeaking.
the sudden death of a child
is an awful fact.
good thing i did my big shopping early.
my timing was always perfect.

Notes

"Living as a Lesbian Underground, ii": The line "memory is your only redemption" is taken from a talk given by Luisa Valenzuela in 1987 at New York University.

"Greta Garbo": Thanks to Mr. Lee Dobson, New York City actor, for the story behind the line "Please, do you have men's pajamas?"

Parts of "Movement" are influenced by Taylor Branch's *Parting the Waters: America During the King Years* (New York: Simon & Schuster, 1988), John Blassingame's *Slave Testimony* (Baton Rouge: Louisiana State University Press, 1977), and *The Life of Olaudah Equiano* in *The Classic Slave Narratives* edited by Henry Louis Gates, Jr. (New York: New American Library, 1987).

"Flowers of Puerto Rico": Epigram by Frances E.W. Harper from "Black Women in the Reconstruction South" in *Black Women in White America: A Documentary History* edited by Gerda Lerner (New York: Vintage Books, 1973); "ii. Reina de las Flores": Influenced by Adrienne Kennedy's *Electra* in *In One Act* (Minneapolis: University of Minnesota Press, 1988).

"Hanging Tough in the Persian Gulf": "For Some Military Presented a Path To College Degree." *The Washington Post*, Sunday, March 10, 1991, p. A22.

Other titles from Firebrand Books include:

My Mama's Dead Squirrel, Lesbian Essays on Southern Culture by Mab Segrest/$9.95

New, Improved! Dykes To Watch Out For, Cartoons by Alison Bechdel/$7.95

The Other Sappho, A Novel by Ellen Frye/$8.95

Out In The World, International Lesbian Organizing by Shelley Anderson/$4.95

Politics Of The Heart, A Lesbian Parenting Anthology edited by Sandra Pollack and Jeanne Vaughn/$12.95

Presenting. . . Sister NoBlues by Hattie Gossett/$8.95

Rebellion, Essays 1980-1991 by Minnie Bruce Pratt/$10.95

Restoring The Color Of Roses by Barrie Jean Borich/$9.95

A Restricted Country by Joan Nestle/$9.95

Running Fiercely Toward A High Thin Sound, A Novel by Judith Katz/$9.95

Sacred Space by Geraldine Hatch Hanon/$9.95

Sanctuary, A Journey by Judith McDaniel/$7.95

Sans Souci, And Other Stories by Dionne Brand/$8.95

Scuttlebutt, A Novel by Jana Williams/$8.95

Shoulders, A Novel by Georgia Cotrell/$8.95

Simple Songs, Stories by Vickie Sears/$8.95

Spawn Of Dykes To Watch Out For, Cartoons by Alison Bechdel/$8.95

Speaking Dreams, Science Fiction by Severna Park/$9.95

Stone Butch Blues, A Novel by Leslie Feinberg/$10.95

The Sun Is Not Merciful, Short Stories by Anna Lee Walters/$8.95

Talking Indian, Reflections on Survival and Writing by Anna Lee Walters/$10.95

Tender Warriors, A Novel by Rachel Guido deVries/$8.95

This Is About Incest by Margaret Randall/$8.95

The Threshing Floor, Short Stories by Barbara Burford/$7.95

Trash, Stories by Dorothy Allison/$9.95

We Say We Love Each Other, Poetry by Minnie Bruce Pratt/$8.95

The Women Who Hate Me, Poetry by Dorothy Allison/$8.95

Words To The Wise, A Writer's Guide to Feminist and Lesbian Periodicals & Publishers by Andrea Fleck Clardy/$5.95

The Worry Girl, Stories from a Childhood by Andrea Freud Loewenstein/$8.95

Yours In Struggle, Three Feminist Perspectives on Anti-Semitism and Racism by Elly Bulkin, Minnie Bruce Pratt, and Barbara Smith/$8.95

You can buy Firebrand titles at your bookstore, or order them directly from the publisher (141 The Commons, Ithaca, New York 14850, 607-272-0000).

Please include $2.00 shipping for the first book and $.50 for each additional book.

A free catalog is available on request.